Machines with

Monster Trucks

by Amy McDonald

BLASTOFF!
Beginners

BELLWETHER MEDIA
MINNEAPOLIS, MN

Blastoff! Beginners are developed by literacy experts and educators to meet the needs of early readers. These engaging informational texts support young children as they begin reading about their world. Through simple language and high frequency words paired with crisp, colorful photos, Blastoff! Beginners launch young readers into the universe of independent reading.

Blastoff! Universe

Reading Level — Grade K
Grades 1-3
Grade 4

Sight Words in This Book 🔍

a	have	the
are	is	they
big	it	this
can	jump	yes
do	make	
go	on	

This edition first published in 2021 by Bellwether Media, Inc.

No part of this publication may be reproduced in whole or in part without written permission of the publisher. For information regarding permission, write to Bellwether Media, Inc., Attention: Permissions Department, 6012 Blue Circle Drive, Minnetonka, MN 55343.

Library of Congress Cataloging-in-Publication Data

Names: McDonald, Amy, 1985- author.
Title: Monster trucks / by Amy McDonald.
Description: Minneapolis, MN : Bellwether Media, 2021. | Series: Blastoff! Beginners: Machines with Power! | Includes bibliographical references and index. | Audience: Ages PreK-2 | Audience: Grades K-1
Identifiers: LCCN 2020007092 (print) | LCCN 2020007093 (ebook) | ISBN 9781644873212 (library binding) | ISBN 9781681038087 (paperback) | ISBN 9781681037844 (ebook)
Subjects: LCSH: Monster trucks--Juvenile literature. | Monster trucks--Parts--Juvenile literature. | CYAC: Monster trucks.
Classification: LCC TL230.5.M58 M34 2021 (print) | LCC TL230.5.M58 (ebook) | DDC 629.224--dc23
LC record available at https://lccn.loc.gov/2020007092
LC ebook record available at https://lccn.loc.gov/2020007093

Text copyright © 2021 by Bellwether Media, Inc. BLASTOFF! BEGINNERS and associated logos are trademarks and/or registered trademarks of Bellwether Media, Inc.

Editor: Christina Leaf   Designer: Andrea Schneider

Printed in the United States of America, North Mankato, MN.

Table of Contents

What Are Monster Trucks?

Can trucks jump? Can they **crush** cars? Yes!

Monster trucks
are big machines.
They can
do tricks.

jump

donut

crush cars

Parts of a Monster Truck

Monster trucks have tall wheels. They can drive over cars.

wheels

Monster trucks have a big **engine**. It makes the truck go.

engine

Monster trucks have a **cab**. It keeps the driver safe.

cab

Monster trucks
have names.
The name is
on the body.

body

name

Monster Truck Tricks

This is Iron Man.
It can jump far.

This is Dragon.
It can do
a **donut**.

donut

This is Bigfoot.
It can crush cars.
Crunch!

crushed cars

Monster Truck Facts

Monster Truck Parts

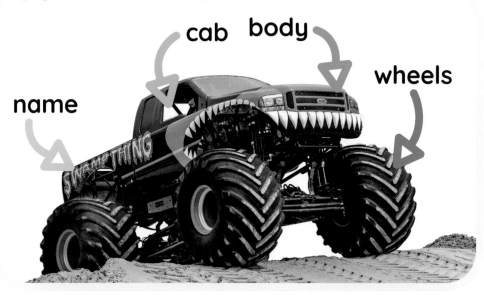

cab body

wheels

name

Monster Truck Tricks

jump   donut   crush cars

Glossary

cab

a place for the driver

crush

to flatten

donut

a spin trick

engine

a part that makes trucks go

To Learn More

ON THE WEB

FACTSURFER

Factsurfer.com gives you a safe, fun way to find more information.

1. Go to www.factsurfer.com.

2. Enter "monster trucks" into the search box and click 🔍.

3. Select your book cover to see a list of related content.

Index

The images in this book are reproduced through the courtesy of: Nigel Jarvis, front cover, p. 3; Dan Hanscom, pp. 4-5; Will Bailey/ Alamy Stock Photo, pp. 6-7; BW Press, pp. 6 (jump), 22 (donut); Melinda Nagy, p. 7 (crush cars); Paul Stringer, pp. 7 (donut), 23 (donut); PhotoStock10, pp. 8-9; PCN Photography, pp. 10 (inset), 23 (engine); Ahry/ Alamy Stock Photo, pp. 10-11; Michael Stokes, pp. 12-13, 23 (crush); Maksim Shmelijov, pp. 14-15; Piotr Zajac/ Alamy Stock Photo, p. 16, 16-17; Hugh Peterswald/ Alamy Stock Photo, pp. 18-19; Simon Bratt, p. 20 (crushed cars); Glyn Thomas/ Age Fotostock, pp. 20-21; Tony Watson/ Alamy Stock Photo, p. 22 (jump); Kutt Niinepuu, p. 22 (crush cars); Dreamstime.com, p. 23 (cab).